All rights reserved with the author.
No public performance or
recording without express permission
of the publisher.

For more publications and
audio/visual catalogue head to:

Instagram –Seasores_njw
YouTube --Seasores N J W
Website --Seasores.com
Contact at--nickjohnwood@mail.com

ISBN: 9798674983507

© 2020.

Foreword

Ten percent of profits I make from this book will be rounded up and donated to the Soi dog foundation. They are a charity dedicated to animal welfare on the ground in Asia.

Soi Dog
Foundation –
Ending the Suffering of Animals in Asia

Please check out their work at
https://www.soidog.org

I've seen first-hand what incredible lengths they go in order to rescue, treat and rehome animals in need, especially saving many dogs from the meat trade.

They work tirelessly in difficult conditions to raise awareness and give second chances to thousands of animals.

If you don't believe dogs can smile, you need go visit their rescue shelter or meet any one of the thousands of pets they've saved and rehomed all around the world.

This small publication is dedicated to the staff and volunteers there.

They need volunteers and good forever homes. Please check out their work and get involved, you won't regret it.

WRITTEN IN THE YEAR OF MASKS,
THIS IS MY SMALL CONTRIBUTION IN THE
EFFORT TO SEE OUR SMILES AGAIN.

FIVE HUNDRED ESSENTIAL ELEMENTS OF
JUST THAT, ENCOURAGING OPTIMISM
ABOUT TOMORROW, THROUGH THE
SIMPLE PLEASURES OF TODAY.

 N J WOOD

The Essential Elements Of A Smile

N J Wood

1. *Lipstick behind the mask.*

2. *The tiny pencil marks running up the wallpaper, indicating the growing child's height.*

3. *Venus rising as the sun sets.*

4. *The second breath after slipping on black ice and realising you didn't fall.*

5. *The nail tacks in the corners of living rooms and halls, on which the Christmas lights will be strung.*

6. *A lungful of creations coming from the kitchen.*

7. *Sitting in the one section of the garden which the sun never quite leaves in winter.*

8. *A small house with a field of roses and peaches, whose owners said no to the developer's dollar.*

9. *Beginning the night in a room filled with strangers, ending it in one full of friends.*

10. *Walking past the neighbour's dog without it barking for the first time.*

11. *The unexpected dragonfly far from water.*

12. *The children waiting to hear if their school is closed on a snow day.*

13. *Savouring the first sip* of coffee as you slowly wake up. That warm feeling.

14. *When the trolly is gone, the shopping's done, bags unpacked and the cupboards full and it's time to treat yourself.*

15. *The scarlet flare of holly berries in the leafless wood.*

16. *Walking barefoot in a downland stream.*

17. *'I love you' someone scratched in the Perspex of the bus shelter.*

+ drops hanging of branches & leaves after the rain

18. *The stack of breadcrumbs and crusts upon a window ledge, saved for the birds.*

19. *The date she circled on the calendar.*

20. *Buying flowers at dusk to give without cause or occasion.*

21. *Your phone reading 'next alarm Monday 7am' at 7pm on a Friday evening.*

22. *Breathing the first scent of sun cream in spring.*

23. *Knocking on the coach door to catch the driver's eye and them slowing to let you on.*

24. *Mountains suited in moonlight and snow.*

25. *The last step reached after the arduous climb and the far-reaching view from the top.*

26. *Candy floss melting on the tongue.*

27. *People who still have landlines and announce their number when you've just called it.*

28. *Thunderstorms shaking walls by midnight, but the horizon clear by dawn.*

29. *Having one hour extra in bed cause the clocks turned back not forward.*

30. *A low line of hills a morning's walk away, through cow parsley and poppy lined lanes.*

31. *A man twice my age swimming out into the ocean, double the distance I ever could.*

32. *Hiding behind the sofa and waiting to say 'Boo!'*

33. *The swallows returning to eves of roofs, they travelled three thousand miles to reach.*

34. *An impromptu barbeque on Brighton beach.*

35. *The white wall flowers growing straight from the sea cliffs.*

36. *Mist making any place a little more magic.*

37. *Exploring through boxes in the attic.*

38. *The sound of French children being French kids in the street.*

39. *The rush of evening heat as the office door opens.*

40. *The faded slogans on the sides of old buildings, like 'Clapham and Sons — Women's Haberdashery'.*

41.   *Desserts before dinner.*

42.   *The perfume of a stranger two places in front.*

43.   *The sound of fingers breaking through chocolate Easter eggs.*

44.   *Meeting grocery brands from home on foreign store shelves.*

45.   *The busting of bubbles as you lower inch by inch into the steaming bath.*

46.   *Cabinets in lounges where children's awards from races won and exams passed are kept on show.*

47. *The first time you know they understood, when speaking their language.*

48. *The unexpected compliment after meeting a cantankerous relative.*

49. *Something broken working again, all on its own.*

50. *The shops filled with stationary each September and wondering what all those pens and pencils will draw.*

51. *Reaching the fun part of your lunch box (Postman Pat).*

52. *The Christmas presents stacked on the wardrobe in November.*

53. *Friends* episodes warming the embers at the end of a hard day.

54. Wooden sticks to eat ice cream from tiny tubs.

55. Realising you share a love for the same movie.

56. Photos of Earth taken from Mars.

57. Traveling far for the person, not the place.

58. The favourite window chair becoming free, while you wait for your order.

59. How a sudden downpour can unite a group of strangers, as they shelter from it

60. Having more in your account than you thought.

61. The first click of the kettle after arriving home from holiday (and how you go away from home, to know how much you want to be there).

62. Third portions at all you can eat buffets.

63. Sincere forgiveness received or given.

64. The things the world shows only after the leaves have fallen.

65. *How high old men's trousers are worn and how high I'm going to wear them.*

66. *The uncrossing of arms through a conversation's length.*

67. *The feast of the morning breakfast table laid out as you go to bed with a mint tea (or fireball whisky).*

68. *Village pub fireplaces and the thousand straggly dogs which sleep beside them.*

69. *Tapas on the terrace.*

70. *Friendships surviving since the first day of school.*

3. Friendships surviving the test of time

71. How love rules over death.

72. Getting a drink at six a.m. seeming to be acceptable in an airport.

73. When a crowd goes 'Ooooo,,' in unison.

74. Receiving kindness again when you most probably didn't deserve it.

75. Showing kindness even though they most probably didn't deserve it.

76. Children's obsessions with stickers never going out of fashion.

5. THAT warm feeling after helping out someone

77. *Passions which traverse the day – tip to toe.*

78. *Forsaking the cosy covers to be out at dawn, though no-one is asking you to be there.*

79. *Reaching your favourite bench in the park.*

80. *Promenades on the promontory, despite the gales and arriving safe to the tea shop door.*

81. *The silent vibe of your living room late at night.*

82. *A table laid and waiting, right before the bell rings.*

83. Leaving a light on for the next to enter.

84. Children's productions of plays - bad accents, acting and false moustaches.

85. Breakfast morning TV on a day off.

86. Discovering you can be happier at work than not.

87. The unknown number texting, 'hey what's up?'

88. Those who discover art late in life.

89. When you hear a sound so often you 'start to stop' hearing it at all.

90. *The brief flicker of porch lamps and dining rooms as you drive past in the evening.*

91. *When the weather gets so bad that the sky darkens like dusk at mid-day.*

92. *A web of city streetlights seen from an aircraft.*

93. *Being 'snug' - when the weather reminds you you're warmer together than apart.*

94. *Boisterous board games on carpets.*

95. The first time each year you take a coffee and they pass it you in a festive cup.

96. Rewarding yourself with a little retail therapy.

97. Alleyways to beaches a shoulder's width wide.

98. The intense turquoise of Mediterranean tides.

99. Irish eyes.

100. Animals in the deepest oceans and darkest forests that science hasn't yet discovered.

101. *Stepping stones across ponds (and rock gardens with ferns unfurling).*

102. *The warm atmosphere of lighting shops.*

103. *Birdsong at night.*

104. *Admiring the dedication of a friend when they complete Ramadan.*

105. *The noisy neighbors letting the world know what it is to be in love.*

106. *Sunlight and a hot mug on the backsteps, when you just need to take five.*

107. The secret places people hide their keys in the garden, under the pot, stone, or fishing Knome.

108. Children asking adults to act like grownups.

109. The inheritance of things of no value, which are the most valuable things you own.

110. How the French say 'Ayyy!' rather than 'Ouch!' when they hurt themselves.

111. Keeping alive the traditions of grandparents.

112. *The fat wedge of chocolate in the base of cornetto ice-cream cones.*

113. *Gathering blackberries and blueberries from hedgerows.*

114. *The smell of hardware stores (could only be me).*

115. *Handpicked herbs from the window box*

116. *All the 'firsts' – words, steps, the firsts you don't forget.*

117. *Blaming your character flaws on your star sign (then being told it's probably your rising moon).*

118. *Government U turns after local action (saving the post office).*

119. *Hushed excitement in the auditorium at six fifty-eight and you've got some good seats this time.*

120. *Hearing songs parents listened to when you were a kid and realising, they weren't all that bad after all.*

121. *Piggyback riding at any age.*

122. *The forgotten cash in the back pocket of jeans.*

123. *The names of children's teddy bears (Popcorn Honey Wood).*

124. Having dozens of flavours to pick from.

125. A coffee pot and buns in the meeting room when you are twenty minutes early and you've skipped breakfast.

126. The faces of folks using automatic massage chairs in malls.

127. Initialled handkerchiefs.

128. Icicles from drainpipes.

129. The plastic weapons of Star Wars toys.

130. Suburban flower beds in June and what they say about their owners.

131.   Collecting driftwood and seashells at any age.

132.   Waterfalls cascading down the hillside.

133.   Identifying constellations beside the apple of your eye.

134.   The smell of fresh wood polish.

135.   Christmas markets in scarf and glove.

136.   Boarding passes in passports and the page with all the rubber stamps.

137. *Seeing the waves beneath your feet through the planks of the pier.*

138. *Landscape paintings on biscuit tins, giving it a shake and hearing an unexpected rattle.*

139. *Those front rooms filled with obscure lifelong collections.*

140. *Shoe size measuring machines for kids.*

141. *Jet trails across blue sky – wondering where it's going and if someone is looking back.*

142. *Reaching the eighth stage of grief.*

143. Ghost stories when seated at firesides on winter evenings.

144. Half-arsed happy birthday renditions and the one relative who sings like it's a performance at the Albert Hall.

145. If my Classical collections can shuffle play into my hip-hop and blue grass country music on Spotify without any problems, then there's hope we can all get along.

146. Christmas landing in the middle of Summer down under.

147. Thinking about what happened to your New Year's resolutions in July.

148. The way cats tuck their paws in and close their eyes like little gurus.

149. Speaking highly of someone when they'll never know you have.

150. When being foolish isn't that foolish.

151. How every hotel room has a picture of Paris

152. Turning your sword into a staff.

153. Whispered words.

154. Getting away with swapping Mum's spirits for water without her noticing as a teenager.

155. *Playing hide & seek and not being found and then never telling anyone where you hid.*

156. *The first day you can wear shorts and the first one you can wear long sleeved sweaters again.*

157. *The unexpected balloon burst.*

158. *The lifelong loyalty of swans.*

159. *The difference roof gardens and flower boxes make.*

160. *How honeybees communicate by dancing.*

161.   The wind passing along the tops of hillside trees, one after the next.

162.   Carols by candlelight and cutting ivy to drape behind picture frames.

163.   The sensation of elevators in movement.

164.   When an old man walks in time with the music.

165.   Looking at your town from afar and recognising the outline of your roof or a chimney you know.

166.   Slowly climbing spiral staircases.

167. *A maze of clipped box hedges, their hand leading you in and not caring much if you ever make it out.*

168. *People you wouldn't expect having secret tattoos.*

169. *The times the birds all choose to sing when far from dawn and yet nowhere near dusk.*

170. *Your phone being found and returned by a good-hearted stranger.*

171. *When trains run parallel to roads and rivers.*

172. *The silver shimmer of old olive groves in the Mistral wind.*

173.   Stone steps worn down in the middle.

174.   Big doors with little doors inside them.

175.   Clothes strewn out upon the floor.

176.   Secret drawers in old cabinets.

177.   Feeling like you've met them before.

178.   Listening to your gut again and it being right.

179.   Diets which always start tomorrow.

180. Souvenir shopping for wooden boats and fridge magnets.

181. Digging holes in the flower bed all the way to China with my nephew.

182. Carving your initials on all the worlds that have ever been and all the worlds that ever will be.

183. The fascinating lives of the little figures in my dad's architecture models.

184. Hidden hordes of lost gold under wheat fields, still awaiting to be found.

185. The sound umbrellas make when they open and close.

186. Waving through a train window as the carriage pulls up.

187. Kite flying in Autumn.

188. Canal boats with a pet or two on deck.

189. Parents getting street slang two years after it fell out of use.

190. Chocolate Christmas decorations and finding one everyone else had missed.

191. The pet wrapping themselves as close to you as they can.

192. Old junk turning out to be one of a kind.

193. Finding a four-leaf clover.

194. Revealing jelly from a mould in one piece.

195. Overly dramatic safety signs.

196. No matter what the museum is about, there's always dinosaurs in the gift shop.

197. Narrow side allies with someone's front door halfway along.

198. The scent of Geraniums in a greenhouse.

199. Rediscovering something you hadn't realised you'd lost.

200. The feeling of glasses resting on your nose when they are no longer there.

201. Roses planted by a lost loved one flowering in May.

202. The foreign coins gathering in the second drawer down after vacations.

203. Willpower occasionally winning out.

204. Your song coming on the radio.

205. *Sleep getting things in order in a way you never could.*

206. *The ice cliffs of Antarctica and a whole continent with almost no-one on it.*

207. *How the Brits and Americans can't agree about apostrophes.*

208. *The desserts only your grandparents made.*

209. *Stick figures in margins.*

210. *Ice cream tubs filled with toys.*

211. *Your ego taking a back seat and learning to love, without want of reward.*

212. *The smell of food as you walk towards a closed door and the key about to turn.*

213. *The first icy breath of winter in mid-October.*

214. *Being schooled in good behaviour by a seven-year-old.*

215. *The gold ring worn by another in your childhood which now never leaves your finger.*

216. *Being out on the waves and how far away the world soon becomes.*

217. *Finally finding the village shop after going round in circles.*

218. *The teenage relative greeting you with unexpected confidence and realising a corner has been turned in their life.*

219. *Building paper boats for woodland streams.*

220. *How kids charge into the sea.*

221. *Labels written in inks and Parcels tied with string.*

222. Giving up calorie counting for Christmas and Boston cream cake.

223. The names grandparents make up for themselves to avoid being called grandpa or grandma.

224. Gargoyles on old churches.

225. The warmth of a conservatory and patience of growing plants from seed.

226. The morning mirror being unexpectedly kind.

227. Breaking fresh pond ice with stones.

228. The hand on the steering wheel of the pickup truck slowing to gesture you can cross.

229. Seeing a kid give up their seat on a crowded train.

230. The searching through a chocolate box, freezer or cupboard and finding goodies you had forgotten were there.

231. The lilac flowering in a sea of concrete.

232. The doors of Fairy houses amid tree roots.

233. Freshly squeezed fruit juice and ice.

234. Watching the sky on Christmas Eve for reindeer.

235. Hating Shakespeare as a child then realising what all the fuss is about.

236. Saying 'Bless you,' when a stranger sneezes and them saying 'Thanks'.

237. Seasonal soups and good bread.

238. That the shooting star you will see in years to come is out there now on course to your eye.

239. Trees fallen in gales still growing years afterwards.

240. The caves the size of Cathedrals.

241. *That one of our descendants will remember us.*

242. *The last step into the landing and the bedroom door handle after everything is done.*

243. *The shirt unworn for a long while that once on, still has the scent of her washing powder.*

244. *The small area around the tree which remains dry as the heavens open.*

245. *Waving at strangers for no particular reason and occasionally them waving back.*

246. Hibernating field mice in the hollows of old trees through Winter (no-one will see).

247. That one streetlamp deciding to remain on all day.

248. Wondering into a wide wheat field.

249. Somewhere out there is a party in a countryside villa, with statues and fountains and music and laughter.

250. Wild grasses in the wind.

251. It being customary to say 'hello,' to strangers you pass on villages paths.

252.   Pink hot water bottles and eiderdown blankets on the coldest nights of the years.

253.   That first hour of feeling a little better after an illness which kept you in bed for days.

254.   The potter's thumb marks in fired clay.

255.   Faces reflected in coloured Christmas baubles

256.   The pigeon perched on the dower faced Victorian statue's hat.

257.   The pen written adverts in the windows of corner stores.

258. The courteous bicycle bell rung before going around a blind bend.

259. Sitting outside the bank and pretending to be the getaway car.

260. That shoe box which holds all the memories.

261. Finding the space in the packed parking lot that no-one else saw.

262. The marriage of cake and ice cream still going strong.

263. The day Christmas decorations appear in the shops.

264. *Dormant buds finally breaking and knowing the thaw has begun.*

265. *Catching it mid-air.*

266. *Being inside the store and watching passers-by checking themselves out in the reflection.*

267. *When you realise that random cup has graduated to become your favourite mug.*

268. *The wit of sports crowds.*

269. *Thatched roofs bowing in the middle, after centuries of midnight snow, evening rain and Summer sun.*

270. The strange feeling inside when the car goes over a small bridge.

271. Learning to live without perfection.

272. Flower shows and cake stands on village greens.

273. Receiving an enveloped invitation on paper like a secret agent.

274. A mid-Summer sun reaching the north facing wall.

275. Times Square on New Year's Eve.

276. The scent of soap on dry hands.

277. The word 'cul-de-sac'.

278.   When a negative result is a positive one.

279.   Letters of acceptance.

280.   Looking behind you to see who may need a hand up.

281.   Resisting blaming others for my own failings.

282.   Blank notebooks.

283.   The migration of butterflies.

284.   Six-foot canvases in Tate Britain.

285. Crocus growing in clumps through suburban lawns each February.

286. Carved stone dates above doorways.

287. Finally finding a word that wouldn't leave the tip of your tongue.

288. Shining a powerful torch into the night sky and watching it reach up into the stars.

289. Being five years old and thinking that a police checkpoint was where the police just checked if you're ok.

290. Sleeping in the shade after a picnic and no rush to go anywhere.

291.   Kids whose favourite colour is black.

292.   Seeing the flash of a tale tail fin through the waves.

293.   The taste of stamps on your tongue.

294.   After trying half a dozen other - finally finding the key that opens the lock.

295.   Pumpkin picking in wellington boots.

296.   The cool expressions of kids in child-seats on the back of bicycles

297. *Meeting rescue animals and the saints who saved them.*

298. *The Sunday roast gathering pace through the morning, parsnips, potatoes, mint and cranberry sauce, gravy pouring over dumplings and a rumbling stomach as the Yorkshire pudding arrives.*

299. *That you say candy and we say sweets.*

300. *Wondering around the rando store just to use their aircon.*

301. *Jogging around a moonlit park and meeting plenty of other joggers.*

302. Those who go out to buy breakfast from the local store still wearing pyjamas.

303. When snow reaches double digit depths and the things we use as a sledge.

304. The wild animal untroubled by your presence but knowing you're there.

305. The swirls of hair on a baby's head.

306. Finger painting Fridays - Wiggling Wednesday's - Snakes and Ladders Saturdays and the endless list of things

parents create to distract and entertain bored sprogs.

307. Laughter in any language.

308. Finally getting the shoes you couldn't afford.

309. Peering into the hot take-away bag.

310. Impromptu shadow puppets.

311. The first lick to the last.

312. The courage to ask for help.

313. The ten-year-old me seeing castle battlements through the trees.

314.   Old friends in the amateur leagues.

315.   Winning the raffle.

316.   The sound wicker chairs make when you sit on them.

317.   The smell of a world which knew nothing but sun for weeks after a Summer downpour.

318.   'Good morning' texts the day after the night before.

319.   Realising you've walked in the wrong direction but keeping going until no-one's there to see you stop and turn.

320. Meeting the person that you can't wait to see at the arrivals' gate.

321. The carving of the pumpkin, lighting the candle without burning your finger and feeling a little pride as said masterpiece sits on the porch.

322. Exploring a fruit orchard in full blossom.

323. The unexpected wink.

324. Thinking it was later than it is and realising you've got hours to play with.

325. *Kids living in a world where everything from the sun to their food is gallowed to have a smiling face.*

326. *How birds always have some place important to be.*

327. *How it's not the big steps which you can see, but the tiny ones you don't even notice that trip us up.*

328. *The babies being born right now starting out on a long road.*

329. *How some days the eyes of puplic sculptures seem to be looking straight at you.*

330. How smooth an ironed shirt feels when first put on.

331. When 'no-one's left' means – they all stayed, rather than they've all gone.

332. The wedding reception hall prepared and waiting for the first guest.

333. People who say, 'they're a hot mess'.

334. The hand which lifts you up when it could have thrown you down.

335. Baked bread, ground coffee, handpicked fruits and home grown veg — or buying it all from Whole foods

and pretending it's all your hard labour.

336. *Lands which belong solely to seabirds.*

337. *The opening hours of Spanish bakeries.*

338. *Songs in showers, heard by the whole street.*

339. *A serious person's shoe squeaking.*

340. *Stalagmites and stalactites finally meeting.*

341. *The Disney movies they're starting production on today.*

342. Staying longer than you had to and visiting those who don't get visitors.

343. People who have little, but offer much.

344. Love growing at the speed of healing cuts.

345. Looking close-up and seeing the separate strands of colour in a single brush stroke.

346. Landing to see the handwritten notes of airport drivers, with the anticipation on their faces that it might be you.

347. *The $10,000 Rolex and the $10 Casio both telling the same time.*

348. *When sunlight falls along the narrowest of roads.*

349. *Finally finding the darn remote.*

350. *Hope in all and all in hope.*

351. *Passing on a boat beneath a bridge.*

352. *Knowing someone, somewhere, someplace is proposing.*

353. *Elementary school kids starting to make Christmas decorations in November.*

354. *The magic of miniature railways and small details which make all the difference.*

355. *Seventies' rock bands still performing in their seventies.*

356. *The way men ease into grumpiness so slowly they don't even notice.*

357. *Grandparents coming to watch their grandkids play sports.*

358. *The rewarding company of a loyal pet.*

359. *How mad they get if you call them comic books rather than graphic novels.*

360. *Debating if it's arms or legs that octopuses have.*

361. *A good excuse to wear a new suit for the first time.*

362. *The dance we do when trying to waft a persistent fly away.*

363. *The first car of the teenager in the driveway.*

364. *The leaves of last Summer making a fine home for hedgehogs.*

365. *Old maps which say, 'here be monsters!'*

366. The dying art of penny sweets in paper bags.

367. Standing up straight despite the loss with dignity, despite the indignity of it.

368. Last minute reprieves for unloved buildings.

369. Believing the beauty of your future will be greater than the ugliness of your past.

370. Roads whose tree branches touch overhead.

371. Making merry like you're in a Charles Dickens movie.

372.   What kids ask for in supermarkets.

373.   Cinnamon and cloves.

374.   Descending a long elevator as someone is ascending in the opposite direction, all the way.

375.   Second-hand book shop shelves and one dog-eared copy which speaks to you.

376.   The closing of the book a few moments before sleep.

377.   A daughter reaching up to hold the hand of her father.

378. Music remembering where you last heard it.

379. Public hanging baskets on streetlamps.

380. Those trees on the hills that are shaped by the wind

381. The way dust moves in a shaft of sunlight.

382. Those who ride mopeds in suits.

383. The self-satisfaction of shopping for Christmas presents in September.

384. The boss calling in sick.

385. Moss on stones.

386. Age catching up with you but making sure it's out of breath by the time it does.

387. Small acts of corporate rebellion.

388. Weather houses and cuckoo clocks.

389. A record player on a rooftop.

390. The train journey that will take you all day and all the way across the country.

391. Dishes named after places (Black Forest gateau).

392.   How big the school playing field once seemed.

393.   Coloured bows in hairs and babies carried in back pouches.

394.   Revealing the second layer of the chocolate box.

395.   The fox going about their business in daylight.

396.   Nuns traveling in packs.

397.   The unexpected message from your ex and the satisfaction of ignoring it

.

398. Covered arcades of small local shops.

399. Picking up the phone after it's been dropped and realising it's still in one piece.

400. The smell of bakeries at seven in the morning.

401. A ten-year-old thinking they've got this world pretty much licked.

402. People who take selfies while meditating.

403. Documentaries getting better with age.

404.   The magnificent museums of capital cities and the eccentric museums of tiny towns.

405.   The chiropractor's click.

406.   The day you realise old people are young people in disguise.

407.   The thumb rubbing dust away.

408.   Handmade cards with robins and a nest.

409.   Making it through the first few months at a new job and no longer being the newbie.

410.   *Walking sticks made of broken tree branches.*

411.   *Miniature furnishings of dolls houses.*

412.   *Mountains of Turkish Delight.*

413.   *Building the business from scratch.*

414.   *Beans, cheese, and toast forever being called an 'Emily' after our eldest.*

415.   *Visiting England just because of Harry Potter.*

416.   *Returning to steps you sat on as a child.*

417.   When clouds in the same sky go in two different directions.

418.   When scars become strengths.

419.   Understanding French, but never the French.

420.   All gold having been born in a supernova, as an antique star died.

421.   Those who play music with eyes closed.

422.   The strange names of primary school teachers.

423.   That way plants pick a particular month to bloom.

424.   Sheets flexing on the laundry line.

425.   Finding the restroom door just in time.

426.   The one sock intent on running away with the washing machine.

427.   Paintings which lay hidden for centuries.

428.   When it's the right time for candles.

429.   Being able to say, 'I told you so' but not saying it.

430.   Towering columns of cloud over suburban rooftops and the farmland

visible from the balconies of tower blocks— the days which define the seasons.

431. *Opening a window to let the insect out unharmed.*

432. *The next season of the best series finally arriving on streaming.*

433. *People calling underwear 'smalls'.*

434. *The cream teas with strawberry jam in garden-centre cafes.*

435. *Bells of two nearby villages ringing at different times and no-one caring.*

436. *The dedication of the season ticket holder.*

437. *The philosophy of 'happy accidents' by Bob Ross.*

438. *Christmas lights that illuminate the room enough so that no other light is needed.*

439. *Anniversaries which come once a decade.*

440. *Homes which have names instead of numbers.*

441. *The first day of Fall when you can smell wood stoves in the air.*

442.   Willpower returned.

443.   Discovering pressed flowers in the pages of an old book.

444.   The early roles of great actors.

445.   Straw hats and cricket matches and the lasting influence of Daisy Duke.

446.   The sound of a horse's hoofs outside your home.

447.   The optimism of old men giving their numbers to twenty something Baristas.

448. Those who put things in alphabetical order.

449. Taking a second to raise a glass to those no longer with us.

450. Impromptu snowball fights with complete strangers.

451. The length of referees' socks.

452. How doctors hate small talk.

453. Any dog, doing anything, anytime, anywhere, amen.

454. Seeing the moment when the streetlamps all turn on.

455. *Knowing how good she looks in that dress.*

456. *Celebrations which cost nothing but mean everything.*

457. *Passing scented oilcandle shop doors.*

458. *How good the world feels after leaving the gym.*

459. *The faces drawn on the inside of whitewashed store windows.*

460. *Seeing sycamore seeds spiralling on the wind in Autumn.*

461. Finishing off the cookie dough from the bowl.

462. Your optimistic nature being handsomely rewarded.

463. The tough guy being a pushover with his kids.

464. Winning the cuddly toy on the pier.

465. Saying cheers in any language.

466. Everything getting lighter in the sun.

467. Paper umbrellas in colourful cocktails.

468. Your favourite character making it through.

469. Cyclists who wear spandex to go round the park.

470. Being first into the darkend movie theatre and having the pick of the seats.

471. Families posing for photos in order of height.

472. Street lights and falling snow.

473. Those who don't know how beautiful they are, being all the more attractive for it.

474. Watching mole hills for the chance of movement.

475. The spare chairs only brought out for big celebrations.

476. Rebuilding the walls stronger than before.

477. School children's backpacks bigger than they are.

478. Seeing a complete stranger twice in one day.

479. Speaking with eyes.

480. How much you can tell about a person by what they put on their fridge door.

481. The sound of suitcase wheels at four in the morning.

482. The piece of paper torn from a napkin with eleven numbers on it.

483. Forgiveness being a medicine which goes both ways.

484. Those children who will change the world without anyone noticing them yet.

485. *Standing at the grave side of those who held you as a child and feeling something which will never die.*

486. *Families running for buses and trains.*

487. *Finally finding your rhythm.*

488. *How revisiting old songs means revisiting the first place you heard them.*

489. *Stop signs shaped like hearts.*

490. *Scars shaped a little like your own.*

491. *Senior citizen honeymoons.*

492.   *A helicopter passing unexpectedly low.*

493.   *Counting Christmas trees on the way home.*

494.   *Clothes strewn upon the floor.*

495.   *Seeing a place you'd only ever watched on TV, with your own eyes.*

496.   *Knowing where you are coming from, before knowing where you're going to.*

497.   *The out-takes in the credits of the film.*

498.   *The satisfaction of the loud click in the knee.*

499.   *Old folks sticking their tongue out in family photos.*

500. You.

At the very least 2020 was a moment to revaluate what happiness is and for myself it was an interesting experience to explore all the simple moments which make life richer, even amid its unavoidable hardships. Regardless of age, location – or even when we live – most of what we can be grateful for remains remarkably similar and curiously familiar to us all.

I hope you enjoyed exploring some of the moments mentioned in this book and if you did – then that's 501 reasons for me to smile.

4. HAVING MET # NEVER FORGET

-Dedicated to MD-

The Original Smile Factory

Printed in Great Britain
by Amazon